RHODODENDRONS

RHODODENDRONS

AN ILLUSTRATED GUIDE TO VARIETIES, CULTIVATION AND CARE, WITH
STEP-BY-STEP INSTRUCTIONS AND OVER 135 BEAUTIFUL PHOTOGRAPHS

Lin Hawthorne

Photography by Peter Anderson

southwater

This edition is published by Southwater
an imprint of Anness Publishing Ltd
info@anness.com
www.southwaterbooks.com
www.annesspublishing.com

If you like the images in this book and would like to investigate
using them for publishing, promotions or advertising, please visit
our website www.practicalpictures.com for more information.

A CIP catalogue record for this book is available from the British Library.

Publisher: Joanna Lorenz
Editor: Simona Hill
Designer: Julie Francis
Production Controller: Ben Worley

PUBLISHER'S NOTE
Although the advice and information in this book are believed to be accurate and true at the time
of going to press, neither the authors nor the publisher can accept any legal responsibility or liability
for any errors or omissions that may have been made nor for any inaccuracies nor for any loss,
harm or injury that comes about from following instructions or advice in this book.

■ HALF TITLE PAGE
'Pink Leopard'
■ FRONTISPIECE
Rhododendrons in bloom
■ TITLE PAGE
'Cary Ann'

■ LEFT
R. cinnabarinum
Roylei Group
■ OPPOSITE LEFT
'Pink Pearl'
■ OPPOSITE RIGHT
'Bruce Brechtbill'
■ OPPOSITE BELOW
R. luteum

Contents

Introduction

*R*hododendrons have fascinated gardeners for centuries, but it was only with the introduction of plants from the Himalayas in the 1850s that their diversity began to be appreciated. Since then, 500–900 species have been identified, excluding the many hybrids and cultivars.

The familiar large-flowered hybrids represent a small proportion of the genus which includes tiny, ground-hugging evergreens and huge, tree-like specimens that reach 30m (100ft) high. Flowers range from the small and delicate to the magnificent and gloriously coloured. But to consider rhododendrons purely as flowering shrubs is to overlook the exquisite new foliage that emerges in some species after flowering. Clothed with fine hair in metallic hues ranging from silver and gold to rich chestnut-bronze, their textural beauty is unsurpassed.

■ RIGHT
Rhododendrons combine well with conifers and other evergreens.

What is a rhododendron?

Rhododendrons constitute an enormous, botanically complex genus of 500–900 species of predominantly evergreen shrubs and trees. They are found scattered throughout the northern temperate regions, extending into South-east Asia. By far the greatest concentration is distributed in the Himalayas of northern India and Burma, in Xinang (Tibet), in South-west China (Guizhou, Yunnan and Sichuan provinces), and in Papua New Guinea; areas which, despite the dangerous terrain and many difficult, long-standing political restrictions, have been a magnet for plant hunters from Victorian times to the present.

A few species, including *R. occidentale*, with azalea-like, creamy white or pink flowers, and the hardy evergreen *R. catawbiense*, with huge trusses of red-purple flowers, occur in North America. In Europe and western Asia, the genus is represented by the hardy, pale-flowered *R. caucasicum* from the Caucasus Mountains, and the vigorous *R. ponticum* which occurs

■ LEFT
R. rex subsp. *arizeleum* is a handsome evergreen with sumptuous flowers varying from clear yellow to deep crimson.

■ RIGHT
The large leaves of *R. falconeri* subsp. *eximium* are typical of those of the Himalayan mountain forests.

around the Mediterranean from Portugal and Spain to Armenia and the Caucasus. This relatively small group of American and European species has proved important in raising many modern hybrids. They have passed on to their offspring the 'iron-clad' or 'hardy hybrid' rhododendrons, a hardy constitution and tolerance of a range of growing conditions that surpass many native Himalayan species. In fact, breeding and selection over the last 150 years have given rise to about 20,000 named cultivars and hybrids.

Growing conditions

The surprising fact about rhododendrons is that they can be found in a wide range of habitats, from harsh arctic tundra at sea level in the case of *R. lapponicum* and *R. camschaticum*, to high alpine meadows in central Europe, above the tree-line in the case of *R. hirsutum*. The arctic and alpine species are mainly compact, low-growing types with small, leathery or hairy leaves. These adaptations are common to many alpine plants, helping them survive the severe climate. Some are intensely fragrant, especially after rain, because the leaves contain aromatic essential oils that act as a kind of cellular anti-freeze. This group includes some of the easiest rhododendrons to grow since they are well-adapted to survive the strong winds and intense light levels typical of high-altitude habitats.

The majority of rhododendrons grow in the moist and humid conditions of massive mountain ranges, where they receive abundant rainfall during their growing season. These include medium-sized species that are native to woodlands close to the tree-line, and the large-leaved, tree-like species such as *R. falconeri* and *R. rex* which dominate in the temperate forest flora that clothe the lower, warmer mountain slopes. In cultivation, these species need shelter and dappled shade with cool humidity and ample moisture in their growing season, like the conditions they experience naturally in their cloud-wrapped mountain home. Rhododendrons grow in peaty, moorland-like soils above the tree-line and in leafy, open, woodland soils rich in decaying organic matter, both being of typically acid nature.

The history of rhododendrons

The name *Rhododendron* is derived from the Greek *rhodos* meaning red, and *dendron* meaning tree, originally applied to the unrelated oleander, *Nerium oleander* with rose-like flowers. The first rhododendron to be named is most likely to have been *R. ferrugineum* with rich, rose-pink flowers; this species is the Alpenrose of the European Alps and Pyrenees. It was introduced to gardens in 1740, although it had been recognized and described long before that date.

Early cultivation

Since the earliest introduction of *R. hirsutum* to European gardens in the mid-1650s, the genus has fascinated plants-people and breeders alike. The arrival of *R. ponticum* in 1763 was an important date in rhododendron history. The huge purple trusses of this hardy species appear to have been universally admired by contemporary gardeners, and the cultivars and hybrids derived from it were considered among the most gorgeous flowering shrubs. As well as being used as an ornamental in its own right, *R. ponticum* was widely planted as game cover throughout Britain and Ireland, and

■ ABOVE
The translucent, blood-red flowers of
***R. thomsonii* can still be seen in many**
modern gardens.

was extensively used as a rootstock for grafting less vigorous but floristically superior forms. Its vigour and tendency to spread rampantly, however, with its ability to render the soil beneath it poisonous to other plant species, is a legacy that can still be seen. Widely naturalized, it is considered a weed in many areas, and in some old gardens it has formed extensive thickets because the

rootstock is more vigorous than the desirable cultivars grafted on to it.

The landmark publication of Joseph Hooker's *Rhododendrons of the Sikkim-Himalayas* (1849–51) made people fully aware of the extraordinary beauty and diversity of

the genus. Sponsored by commercial nurseries and the Royal Botanic Gardens at Kew (then under the directorship of Joseph's father, William Hooker), his expedition to the Himalayas yielded 30 new species of rhododendron, which effectively trebled the number known to cultivation, among them *R. thomsonii* and *R. griffithianum*. Under Joseph Hooker's influence, the cultivation of rhododendrons became a dominant gardening passion of the Victorian period, and many collections that still exist date back to this time. The importance of Hooker's introductions cannot be overestimated.

By the turn of the century, plant collecting in general and rhododendron collecting in particular had become highly competitive. Plant collectors were variously sponsored by wealthy patrons, by the Royal Botanic Gardens at Kew and Edinburgh, by the Arnold Arboretum in Boston, Massachusetts, and by a succession of ambitious nurserymen, including the Veitch Nurseries at Exeter and Bees Nurseries at Liverpool. Arthur Bulley, whose garden at Ness, in Cheshire, England, is now the home of the University of Liverpool's Botanic Garden, was a patron of collecting expeditions by Francis Kingdon-Ward (1885–1958) and Ernest Wilson (1876–1930), both of whom made enormous contributions to the genus in cultivation. Kingdon-Ward, a schoolmaster in Shanghai in 1907, took part in around 20 major expeditions in north-west Yunnan, upper Assam, Burma and Tibet, and was responsible for introducing the species *R. macabeanum* and *R. wardii*, among others.

For gardeners, the legacy of 'Chinese' Wilson, as Ernest Wilson was called, is immense. He also collected in Yunnan and Sichuan for the Veitch Nurseries, and later for the Arnold Arboretum. He brought back

■ LEFT
R. yakushimanum, a compact, dome-shaped bush from Japan, is the parent of many very hardy modern hybrids.

■ LEFT
R. griersonianum introduced vibrant reds into the flowers of many of its hybrid descendants.

■ BELOW
'Hinode-giri', one of Wilson's famous 50 Kurume azaleas, is a compact shrub with exceptionally vivid flowers.

a total of 3,356 new species, of which 900 were new to science, including around 60 rhododendrons. He is perhaps most famous for his collection of 50 Kurume azaleas from Japan, collected in 1914–17. Known as Wilson's Fifty, they include 'Hinode-giri', 'Kumo-no-ito', 'Shin Seikai' and 'Tsuta-momiji'.

From around the turn of the century to 1939, the regions in which the plant collectors worked were subject to great political upheaval, civil war and famine, and many collectors endured not only diseases but severe physical dangers. For example, George Forrest (1873–1932) was at a French mission when Tibetan monks murdered 80 people there. The few surviving members of his party escaped, pursued by hounds.

■ BELOW

'Redshank' is a modern hybrid azalea of a type first bred at Knap Hill and further developed by Rothschild at Exbury.

Modern development

Forrest has been well regarded by botanists up to the present day because of his impeccable, detailed collecting notes; he sent 30,000 specimens from Yunnan, among them 309 reputedly new species of rhododendron.

R. griersonianum is one of the best known and probably the most important because it introduced true reds to the breeding of modern hybrids. In 1915, the thirst for new

species led to the formation of the Rhododendron Society, which sponsored Forrest and others in their search for new species to enhance their breeding programmes. The formation of syndicates by patrons to finance collecting expeditions was a vital aspect of the development of rhododendrons as garden plants.

Many of the best gardens to see rhododendrons were planted in the first quarter of this century by members of this society, notably at Caerhays in Cornwall, Bodnant in

Wales, the Savill Garden in Windsor, and the home of Baron Lionel de Rothschild (1882–1942) at Exbury in Hampshire. Lionel was the first of the Rothschild dynasty to be associated with the genus, and he bred 1,200 hybrids, the best of which are still grown today. At Exbury he devoted 250 acres to the growing of hybrid seedlings, and was ruthless in selecting only those he considered the best, including the well-known Exbury hybrid azaleas.

The dynastic legacy of the Cox family, from Glendoick in Perthshire, is one that stretches back to Euan (E. H. M.) Cox, who collected with Reginald Farrer in upper Burma in 1919. His son Peter and grandson Kenneth continue to collect and to breed rhododendrons, notably their award-winning dwarf rhododendrons, such as 'Ptarmigan' and 'Curlew' that are named after wild birds. These shrubs are bred to withstand the rigours of the north European climate. Many other modern breeders aspire to follow the Cox family's example, for they continue the long tradition of botanical introductions and plant conservation, and produce many beautiful hybrids that most of us, with even the smallest gardens, can delight in growing.

Growing rhododendrons

When growing any rhododendrons, the most important factor for success is to ensure that they have acid soil, preferably with a pH of 4.5–5.5. Many tolerate conditions that are only slightly acid (pH 6); very few will tolerate alkaline soils which contain calcium as chalk or lime.

Soil and moisture

If you have alkaline soil, do not be misled into thinking that you can grow thriving rhododendrons by making a large, deep planting hole and filling it with acidic sphagnum moss peat. This produces only short-term results, because eventually lime in the ground water seeps into the soil. To combat this, you will be committed to long-term, expensive treatment to correct lime-induced chlorosis. Choose plants which suit your soil rather than trying to alter the soil to suit the plants. If you covet rhododendrons but have alkaline soil, grow them in tubs, pots or other large containers.

The ideal soil is an acid, sandy loam that contains copious quantities of humus-rich organic matter; it should be well-drained and moisture-retentive. All rhododendrons need an adequate moisture supply, especially

■ ABOVE
Massed plantings of rhododendrons produce their best flowers and foliage in sheltered, dappled shade beneath an open woodland canopy.

during their growing period and when their flower buds are developing. Few gardens are blessed with ideal conditions, but all soils, be they light or heavy, can be made more suitable by incorporating plenty of organic matter in the form of leaf mould, spent hops, well-rotted manure, or garden compost. Light, sandy soils which dry out very quickly will also need an annual mulch to conserve soil moisture. If your soil is

■ LEFT
New foliage can be sensitive to sun and
wind scorch. Good shelter is essential.

■ BELOW
The haziness of light filtering through
the woodland canopy is caused by the
high levels of atmospheric humidity.

heavy clay, which is cold, wet and
poorly drained, incorporating
organic matter and grit will help
improve matters. If, however,
subsoil drainage is poor, a remedy
is necessar,y because constant damp
will lead to root rot. In severe cases
with wet, very heavy soils, this
usually entails laying land drains,
but in smaller gardens where this
is impractical or unacceptably
expensive, it is worth considering
creating raised beds and filling
them with specially prepared soil.

Shade and shelter

The other major enemies of
rhododendrons are exposure to
cold, dry winds and too much direct
sun, but that is not to say that all
rhododendrons need shade or that
every rhododendron needs protection
from direct sun at all costs. Most
perform best in partial or dappled

Small alpine rhododendrons and their hybrids are displayed to great effect in rock gardens.

removed to create a high canopy, letting in adequate, dappled light but not direct sun. The tree trunks will filter the worst of the winds, but lower, ground-level plantings are also necessary to provide supplementary shelter. Solid screens, such as brick walls, merely create high-speed vortices in their lee, often more damaging than no shelter at all.

Hardy hybrids

The hardy hybrids or 'iron-clad' rhododendrons, on the other hand, have inherited a more robust constitution from their parents. Most will tolerate open sites in sun, provided that their root zone remains reliably moist. They are ideal for most general plantings, and may be grown as specimens, in shrub borders, or as screens and hedging. They even tolerate atmospheric pollution.

The small-leaved alpine species and their hybrid offspring are also quite well-adapted to sun and wind exposure. They are perfect for rock gardens, and can be used in mixed plantings with conifers and heathers. Many will thrive in containers filled with ericaceous (lime-free) compost (soil mix), but they need regular watering if they are to thrive.

shade in a sheltered site, but many tree-like and large-leaved species and their hybrids, especially those from Himalayan forests, do need shade and shelter from wind. If exposed to wind or hot sun, they lose more moisture from the large surface area of their leaves than the roots can readily replenish, and quickly succumb to what is, in effect, a drought. As a general rule, the larger the leaves, the more shelter is required.

If you want to grow these species, they are best in woodland-type conditions, or sited among large trees that have had their lower branches

Azaleas

The Mollis, Knap Hill-Exbury and Occidentale groups of deciduous azaleas (one of the most horticulturally important species of the genus rhododendron) also tolerate sun and warmth; indeed many have better autumn leaf colour in sunny sites. Most of the evergreen azaleas need some shelter from wind, but will tolerate sun. Do bear in mind, however, that those with bright, vibrant flower colours often bleach in strong sunshine; these are best grown in light shade.

Frost tolerance

With the exception of the Indian (Indica) hybrids that are commonly grown as winter-flowering houseplants, all of the plants described in the Plant directory are fully hardy, but the flowers of any rhododendron that blooms before the last of the spring frosts are susceptible to damage. The risk of damage can be reduced by thoughtful siting. Do not plant in low-lying areas that are known to be frost pockets (where cold air collects at the bottom of a slope). In fact, frost damage is most often caused when early morning sun strikes frozen tissues, inducing a rapid thaw that ruptures cell membranes. To avoid this problem, plant where the leaves and flowers receive shade from the early morning sun, so that they can adjust slowly to the increasing day-time temperatures.

Companion plants

As rhododendrons are by nature shallow-rooting, they dislike any underplantings within their root zone which will compete for moisture and nutrients. The type of plants that are likely to succeed as companions are those that occur naturally in similar habitats, such as lilies, *Meconopsis* (Himalayan poppies) and especially ferns and primulas, and other acid-loving members of the family Ericaceae. These plants enjoy light dappled shade with moist, well-drained leafy soil at their roots. Be sure to plant them in groups between specimens, so that they do not encroach on the root zone.

■ LEFT
The hardy hybrids are ideal for general plantings and have good tolerance of sun and exposure.

Classification of rhododendrons

The botanical classification of *Rhododendron*, one of the largest genera in the plant kingdom, is extremely complex, because the genus is divided into eight subgenera which further divide into sections and subsections. For most gardeners, the controversial art of classification has little attraction, for the botanical features that identify a plant with certainty are seldom those that have aesthetic appeal. It is more useful here to categorize them horticulturally.

■ RIGHT
Evergreen rhododendron

Evergreen rhododendrons

These evergreen shrubs and trees range in size from cushion-forming dwarfs to tree-like species that may reach 30m (100ft) in height. This grouping includes most cultivated types which do not fall into other categories, most importantly the 'iron-clad', hardy hybrids derived from *R. catawbiense*, *R. caucasicum* and *R. ponticum*.

Evergreen and deciduous azaleas

These small to medium-sized shrubs with evergreen or deciduous leaves usually have small, often brightly coloured flowers in spring and early summer; the deciduous types frequently have glorious autumn colours. Known by their common name, azalea, and once classified as a separate genus, all now belong to the botanical section *Azalea*.

Deciduous hybrid azaleas

Ghent (Ghandavense) hybrids: raised in Ghent in Belgium in the 1820s from complex crosses between North American azaleas and *R. luteum*. Most are hardy, with scented, single or double flowers in early summer.

■ RIGHT
Azalea-type rhododendron

■ LEFT
A selection of the many flower shapes
which vary from tubular through funnel-,
trumpet- or bell-shaped to star-shaped.

Knap Hill-Exbury hybrids: hardy
English azaleas derived from
American azalea species and *R. molle*.
Medium-sized bushes with large
trusses of brightly coloured flowers
that appear from mid- to late spring.

New Zealand Ilam Hybrids: a more
modern development of the Knap
Hill-Exbury hybrids.

Mollis hybrids: hardy, medium-
sized crosses between *R. molle* and
R. molle subsp. *japonicum*, originating
in Holland and Belgium from 1870
onwards. They bear their funnel-
shaped flowers before the leaves
emerge in late spring.

Occidentale hybrids: grow to 2m
(6½ft) tall; from crossings between
R. occidentale and Mollis hybrids
made in England in the early
1900s. In delicate pastel shades
of pink and white, most are scented,
especially in the evening. Flower
in early summer. Hardy.

Rustica hybrids: compact, hardy,
double-flowered, often sweetly
scented azaleas from crossings made
in the late 19th century between
double-flowered Ghent azaleas and
R. molle subsp. *japonicum*.

Evergreen hybrid azaleas

Most are not strictly evergreen but
have spring leaves and new summer
leaves, lasting at least until the
following spring.

Gable hybrids: bred by Joseph
Gable in Pennsylvania, USA, they
are hardy, late spring- to early
summer-flowering azaleas derived
from *R. kaempferi* and *R. yedoense*
var. *poukhanense*.

Glenn Dale hybrids: from Maryland,
USA, they have complex parentages.
They are hardy and produce showy,
often scented flowers from spring
to summer.

Shammarello hybrids: from north
Ohio, USA, they are exceptionally
hardy, late spring-flowering bushes
derived mainly from *R. yedoense* var.
poukhanense and 'Hino-crimson'.

Kurume hybrids: small, slow-growing
azaleas of Japanese origin involving
R. kiusianum, *R. kaempferi* and *R.
obtusum*. They flower in spring.
Most thrive in sun.

Kyushu hybrids: compact,
exceptionally hardy, small-leaved
plants, raised in Japan from several
dwarf species, including *R. kiusianum*.

Indica hybrids: raised in Belgium
in the 19th century from *R. indica*,
R. simsii and *R. mucronatum*. They
are frost-tender hybrids grown as
winter-flowering houseplants.

Oldhamii hybrids: dwarf, spring-
flowering azaleas raised in England.

Kaempferi hybrids: Dutch, spring-
flowering hybrids which are hardier
than the Kurume azaleas, but like
them, are derived from *R. kaempferi*.

Vuyk hybrids: bred by Vuyk van
Ness in Holland, these are hardy,
showy, late spring-flowering
crosses involving *R. kaempferi*,
R. mucronulatum and Mollis hybrids.

Azaleodendrons: crossings of
deciduous azaleas with evergreen
hybrid rhododendrons.

■ BELOW
Leaf sizes
vary from the
enormous 1m
(3ft) leaves of
R. sinogrande to
the tiniest, as in
R. impeditum.

Plant Directory

Since the genus *Rhododendron* includes 20,000 listed hybrids, any selection must be to some extent arbitrary. This directory represents only a selection of the finest, chosen for their ornamental merits, and includes most types in cultivation today, to suit a range of sites and situations. Heights and spreads cited are those the plants can achieve given good cultivation and ideal growing conditions.

■ ABOVE

'ALISON JOHNSTONE'

(Parents: *cinnabarinum* Concatenans Group x *R. yunnanense*)
A hardy evergreen shrub with neat, elliptic, bluish-green leaves with an attractive lustre. Compact and vigorous habit. Dainty, bell-shaped flowers, tinted peach-pink, are borne in loose trusses in late spring and early summer. Best in sun or light, dappled shade with shelter from cold, dry winds. Height and spread 2m (6½ft).

■ ABOVE

'ARCTIC TERN'

An intergeneric hybrid properly known as x *Ledodendron* 'Arctic Tern'. This is a compact but vigorous, very floriferous evergreen shrub with small trusses of green-tinted white flowers in late spring and early summer. Best in part-shade. Height and spread 60cm (2ft).

■ ABOVE
R. ARGYROPHYLLUM
'CHINESE SILVER'

(Parents: selection of *R. argyrophyllum*
subsp. *nankingense*)
A hardy evergreen shrub of dense,
elegant habit with deep green, lance-
shaped leaves clothed in dense, silver-white
hair beneath. The pale pink, funnel-shaped
flowers are borne in loose trusses in late
spring. Best in dappled shade with shelter.
Height 6m (20ft), spread 2.5m (8½ft).

■ LEFT
R. AUGUSTINII 'ELECTRA'

(Parents: *augustinii* x *R. augustinii*
subsp. *chasmanthum*)
One of the hardy evergreen shrubs raised
by Lionel de Rothschild. It has a tree-like
habit, with lance-shaped dark green leaves
and trusses of funnel-shaped, violet-blue
flowers; they have yellow-green markings
in mid-spring. The blue of the flowers is
most intense in warm seasons. Tolerates
some sun, preferring dappled shade.
Height 4m (13ft), spread 2.5m (8ft).

■ ABOVE
'BASHFUL'

(Parents: 'Doncaster' x
R. yakushimanum)
A hardy Yakushimanum hybrid: an
evergreen wide-spreading shrub with
attractive, red-tinted foliage that has a
silvery lustre when young. The trusses
of funnel-shaped pink flowers have
rust-coloured blotches and become paler,
almost white, with age. Tolerates full sun.
Height to 2m (6½ft), spread 2m (6½ft).

■ LEFT
'BLUE PETER'

Vigorous, free-flowering, evergreen hardy hybrid of rather open, upright habit. The lavender-blue flowers have frilled petals and are white at the throat, with maroon-purple spots; they are borne in dense, conical trusses in late spring and early summer. Tolerates sun. Height to 3m (10ft), spread 3m (10ft).

■ BELOW
'BERRYROSE'

(Knap Hill-Exbury hybrid)
Raised at Exbury by Lionel de Rothschild, this deciduous azalea has copper-tinted young leaves and trusses of delicate, peachy, salmon-pink flowers with a yellow flare in late spring. Good for smaller gardens. Hardy and tolerates sun. Height and spread 1.5m (5ft).

■ ABOVE
'BRUCE BRECHTBILL'

Evergreen shrub of dense habit, bearing large, dome-shaped trusses of pale pink flowers that are yellow at the throat. It flowers in late spring and early summer. A sport of 'Unique', which is a hybrid of *R. campylocarpum*. Height to 1.8m (6ft), spread to 2.5m (8½ft).

■ ABOVE
'CARITA'

(Parents: *R. campylocarpum* x 'Naomi')
Bred at Exbury by Lionel de Rothschild.
A rather columnar shrub of open habit
with elegant, deep rich green foliage.
In mid-spring, trusses of pale lemon-
yellow, funnel-shaped flowers appear on
mahogany-coloured stems. They open
from peach-pink buds to reveal honey
yellow throats with a cerise blotch. Needs
shelter and partial shade. Height 2.5m
(8½ft), spread 2.5m (8½ft) or more.

■ RIGHT
'CARY ANN'

(Parents: 'Corona' x 'Vulcan')
Small, hardy evergreen shrub of compact
habit, with dark green leaves and, from late
spring to early summer, full, rounded
trusses of coral-pink flowers. Good for
smaller gardens. Tolerates some sun.
Height and spread 1.5m (5ft).

■ BELOW
'CHANTICLEER'

A dense, bushy evergreen, this Glenn Dale hybrid azalea has small, dark green leaves, and is noted for its hardiness and relatively large, freely produced flowers. Trusses of scented, funnel-shaped flowers in spectacular maroon-purple appear from late spring to early summer. Tolerates some sun, but the colour is best preserved in dappled shade. Height and spread 1.5m (5ft).

■ ABOVE
'CÉCILE'

Knap Hill-Exbury hybrid azalea bearing rounded trusses with a narrow funnel-shape, which open from deep salmon-pink buds. Flowers are an intense salmon-pink colour with a satin texture and an orange-yellow flare. Flowers for long periods in late spring. Hardy and tolerates sun. Height and spread 2m (6½ft).

■ ABOVE
R. CHARITOPES

A low-growing, compact, evergreen shrub from southern Tibet, with small, aromatic leaves and trusses of waxy, bell-shaped, rose-madder, pale pink or violet flowers which are freely borne in late spring–early summer. Good for a rock garden. When botanists try to identify rhododendrons, they examine the scales beneath the leaves with a hand lens; in this case they are interesting and distinctive, pale green and pink, glistening against a paler background. Height and spread 1m (3ft).

■ ABOVE
R. CINNABARINUM ROYLEI GROUP

A selection of the species introduced by Joseph Hooker from Sikkim. Medium to large-sized evergreen shrub with elliptic leaves that are broader than those of the species, and distinctly blue-tinted when young. The waxy, deep coppery-plum to crimson-coloured flowers appear between mid-spring and early summer. Must have shade and shelter. Hardy to about -10°C (14°F). Height to 6m (20ft), often less, spread 2m (6½ft).

■ ABOVE
'CORNEILLE'

An old, hardy Ghent azalea dating back to about 1890. A small-leaved, deciduous shrub of open, upright habit producing deep pink buds in early summer that open to reveal double, creamy pink, trumpet-shaped flowers with good scent. An elegant specimen that colours well in the autumn. Height and spread 1.5–2.5m (5–8½ft).

■ BELOW
'CYNTHIA'

(Parents: *R. catawbiense* x *R. griffithianum*)
One of the most reliable of the hardy hybrids. In late spring this vigorous evergreen shrub produces enormous conical trusses of rich rose-crimson flowers with crimson-black markings. Tolerates sun. Raised in England in 1870. Height and spread to 6m (20ft).

■ ABOVE
'CURLEW'

(Parents: *R. fletcherianum* 'Yellow Bunting' x *R. ludlowii*)
Dwarf, free-flowering evergreen shrub with small, rich dark green leaves and surprisingly large, funnel-shaped, pale yellow flowers with green-brown markings in mid-spring. Performs best in a cool position. Height and spread 60cm (2ft).

■ LEFT
'DAVIESII'

(Parents: *R. molle* x *R. viscosum*)
A sturdy shrub of suckering habit, this Ghent azalea has excellent autumn colour. In late spring–early summer it produces trusses of wonderfully scented cream flowers that are flushed pink with a golden-orange flare. Height and spread 1.5m (5ft).

■ LEFT
R. DECORUM

Large evergreen shrub of tree-like habit
with decorative bark and dark green leaves.
It bears loose trusses of fragrant, funnel-
shaped, white or pink flowers in early
summer. Hardy and surprisingly tolerant
of sun and warm, dry conditions. Collected
by Ernest Wilson in 1901. Height to 6m
(20ft), spread 2.5m (8½ft).

■ BELOW
'DOPEY'

(Parents: [*R. facetum* x 'Fabia'] x [*R. yakushimanum* x 'Fabia Tangerine']) Small to medium-sized, hardy evergreen shrub of compact, upright habit. In late spring it freely produces neat, dense, rounded trusses of bell-shaped, satiny orange-red flowers with brown markings. Height to 2m (6½ft), spread 2m (6½ft).

■ RIGHT

'EXBURY WHITE'

A deciduous Knap Hill-Exbury azalea with large, white, trumpet-shaped flowers, each with a golden orange-yellow eye, in late spring. It has good autumn colour and is tolerant of heat and sun. An elegant specimen shrub. Height and spread 1.8–2m (6–6½ft).

■ LEFT

'FASTUOSUM FLORE PLENO'

(Parents: *R. catawbiense* x *R. ponticum*)
A hardy hybrid evergreen shrub with a dense, domed habit. It bears rounded trusses of double, funnel-shaped, deep mauve flowers with crimson-brown marks in late spring and early summer. Hardy and tolerant of sun, although the flower colour is best preserved in dappled shade. Height to 4m (13ft), spread 4m (13ft).

■ ABOVE

'GOLDEN TORCH'

(Parents: 'Bambi' x ['Grosclaude' x *R. griersonianum*])
A hardy, free-flowering evergreen hybrid of compact, upright habit, with large trusses of rich salmon-pink buds that open in late spring and early summer to reveal funnel-shaped, pale yellow flowers that later fade to cream. Height to 1.5m (5ft), spread 1.5m (5ft).

■ BELOW
'GRACE SEABROOK'

(Parents: 'Jean Marie de Montague' x
R. strigillosum)
A robust, vigorous, hardy evergreen shrub.
The deep pink flowers, which pale at the
margins, are borne in dense conical trusses,
set off against neatly pointed dark green
leaves, in early–mid-spring. Height to 2m
(6½ft), spread 2m (6½ft).

■ ABOVE
'HATSUGIRI'

Dwarf, small-leaved Kurume azalea of compact habit and hardy constitution.
In spring, the glossy young leaves are obscured by masses of delicate, funnel-
shaped, intense crimson-magenta flowers. Tolerant of sun. Introduced from
Japan about 1915. Height and spread 60cm (2ft).

■ ABOVE
'HYDON DAWN'

(Parents: 'Springbok' x *R. yakushimanum*)
A compact evergreen shrub with semi-glossy dark green leaves
that are clothed in creamy white hairs beneath when young.
The funnel-shaped, pale pink flowers are paler at the wavy petal
margins and are held in compact globular trusses in mid-spring
and early summer. Hardy and tolerant of full sun. Height to 1.5m
(5ft), spread 1.5m (5ft).

■ ABOVE
'HINO-MAYO'

A dense, compact Kurume azalea with
small, shiny green young leaves and dainty,
funnel-shaped, clear pink flowers, in mid-
spring–early summer. Will grow in full
sun. Introduced from Japan, about 1910.
Excellent for small gardens. Height and
spread 60cm (2ft).

■ RIGHT
'HOMEBUSH'

A lovely Knap Hill-Exbury hybrid azalea
introduced in 1926. It has dainty, semi-
double flowers of a distinctive, bright
rose-madder, with paler shading, borne
in dense, round trusses in late spring.
Height to 1.5m (5ft), spread 1.5m (5ft).

■ BELOW
R. IMPEDITUM

This is a dwarf, alpine evergreen shrub
from the mountains of Yunnan and
Sichuan, forming a characteristic low mass
of tangled stems with small, aromatic,
scaly leaves; the scent is especially
noticeable after rain. The funnel-shaped,
almost star-like, pale blue-purple flowers
in mid- to late spring are borne singly
or in pairs. Excellent for rock gardens
and tolerates sun and exposure. Height
to 60cm (2ft), spread 60cm (2ft).

 ABOVE
'HYDON HUNTER'

(Parents: 'Springbok' x *R. yakushimanum*)
A vigorous, compact evergreen with dark green leaves, clothed in
creamy white hairs beneath when young. Produces funnel-shaped,
deep pink flowers spotted orange within in mid-spring and early
summer. Very hardy and tolerant of full sun. Height to 1.5m (5ft),
spread 1.5m (5ft).

■ RIGHT

R. LUTEUM

A species of azalea from the mountains of eastern Europe and the Caucasus, with an open habit and deciduous, lance-shaped leaves. It is extremely fragrant and has been used for breeding other well-scented hybrids. The sweetly scented, funnel-shaped yellow flowers are produced in late spring and early summer, and its autumn colour is exceptional. Prefers full sun. A hardy and elegant shrub. Height to 4m (13ft), spread 4m (13ft).

■ ABOVE

R. KIUSIANUM

Dense, low-growing, evergreen species azalea with small ovate leaves, introduced by Wilson from the high mountains of Kyushu, Japan, in 1918. It is a sun-loving species that produces masses of clustered, funnel-shaped flowers in late spring and early summer, in a colour range from salmon-red to crimson or purple. This is the species from which the Kurume azaleas were developed. Height and spread 1.2m (4ft).

■ RIGHT

'LODER'S WHITE'

(Parents: ['Album Elegans' x *R. griffithianum*] x 'White Pearl') Robust and vigorous, this large-leaved evergreen shrub produces sumptuous trusses of fragrant, funnel-shaped white flowers, flecked with red within, that unfold from neatly furled buds in early to mid-summer. Hardy and tolerant of sun. Height and spread 3m (10ft).

■ BELOW
'MAY DAY'

(Parents: *R. griersonianum* x
R. haematodes)
Low-growing, wide-spreading and
free-flowering evergreen shrub with large
leaves that are velvety and hairy beneath.
The loose, drooping trusses of funnel-
shaped flowers are a rich, glowing scarlet
red. Tolerates sun. Height and spread
1.5m (5ft).

■ LEFT
R. MOUPINENSE

Dwarf evergreen shrub from the
mountains of western China, with glossy
dark green leaves. In late winter and early
spring it produces masses of sweetly
scented, white, soft pink or deep rose-
pink flowers, three per truss. Grow in a
sheltered site because the early flowers are
susceptible to frost damage, but it is so
lovely that it is worth the risk. Introduced
by Wilson in 1909. Height and spread
1.2m (4ft).

■ ABOVE
'MRS C. PEARSON'

(Parents: 'Catawbiense Album' x
'Coombe Royal')
Hardy evergreen shrub of robust, upright
habit, bearing conical trusses of large,
pale mauve-pink flowers, spotted with
chestnut brown, in late spring and early
summer. Height 2m (6½ft), spread 2m
(6½ft) or more.

■ BELOW
'NARCISSIFLORUM'

A vigorous Ghent azalea of compact, upright habit, noted for its delicate, sweetly scented, hose-in-hose (flower within a flower) soft pale yellow flowers, produced in late spring and early summer. The flowers have darker shading on the outside of the petals. Hardy and tolerant of warmth. Raised by Van Houtte, pre-1871. Height to 2.5m (8½ft), spread 2.5m (8½ft).

■ ABOVE
'NAOMI'

(Parents: 'Aurora' x *R. fortunei*)
A handsome, evergreen, tree-like shrub with huge trusses of scented, perfectly formed, funnel-shaped flowers in soft lilac-mauve, faintly marked with brown, in mid-spring. Robust and hardy, it flowers freely once well established. Bred at Exbury by Rothschild in 1926. There is a group of similar, lovely cultivars, such as 'Naomi Exbury' with yellow tints, and 'Naomi Pink Beauty', in rich, deep satin-pink. Height to 5m (16½ft), spread 5m (16½ft).

■ ABOVE
'PALESTRINA'

(Parents: 'J. C. van Tol' x *R. kaempferi* hybrid)
Small-leaved, free-flowering Vuyk azalea of compact, upright habit,
bred in the Netherlands in 1926. It produces trusses of pure white
flowers, faintly marked olive-green at the throat, set against rich
green foliage, in late spring. One of the loveliest hardy evergreen
hybrid azaleas. Height and spread 1.2m (4ft).

■ ABOVE
R. NIVEUM

A gorgeous evergreen species from the
Himalayan woodlands, with felt-like white
shoots and greyish-green leaves clothed
in palest fawn hairs as they emerge.
The perfect trusses of dark-eyed, bell-
shaped flowers in mid-spring are of an
extraordinary dusky blue-purple. Hardy
to -10°C (14°F), but must have shelter
and dappled shade. Height to 6m (20ft),
spread 4m (13ft).

■ LEFT
'PENHEALE BLUE'

(Parents: *R. russatum* x *R. concinnum*
Pseudoyanthinum Group)
Compact, free-flowering evergreen shrub
that is covered in early spring with starry,
glowing violet-blue flowers flushed with
red and red-tinted anthers. Tolerant of sun
and hardy. Height to 1.2m (4ft), spread
1.2m (4ft).

■ ABOVE
'PERSIL'

Knap Hill-Exbury azalea with a neat, bushy habit and funnel-shaped, glistening white flowers with a golden orange blotch, in mid-spring. It was raised in England pre-1925 and given its name in 1945. Height to 2m (6½ft), spread 2m (6½ft).

■ ABOVE
'PERCY WISEMAN'

(Parents: 'Fabia Tangerine' x *R. yakushimanum*)
Compact, hardy evergreen shrub producing, in late spring and early summer, large trusses of peachy pink, funnel-shaped flowers that fade almost to white as they age – a characteristic inherited from the *R. yakushimanum* parent. Tolerant of sun. Height and spread to 1.8m (6ft).

■ LEFT
'PINK PEARL'

(Parents: 'Broughtonii' x 'George Hardy')
A vigorous, popular evergreen shrub that was considered a breakthrough when it was first bred by Waterer's nurseries in 1897, and it has certainly justified early expectations. It has an upright, open habit and becomes rather tree-like as it matures. The huge conical trusses of large, funnel-shaped flowers that appear in mid- to late spring are a lovely soft pink and fade to white as they mature. Hardy and tolerant of sun. Height to 4m (13ft), spread 4m (13ft).

■ RIGHT

'STRAWBERRY ICE'

A hardy, sun-loving Knap Hill-Exbury hybrid azalea bred in 1947. This is a bushy, deciduous shrub with well-filled trusses of funnel-shaped flowers, the colour, as its name suggests, of strawberry sorbet. Height to 2m (6½ft), spread 2m (6½ft).

■ ABOVE

'POLAR BEAR'

(Parents: *R. auriculatum* x
R. diaprepes)

A hardy evergreen shrub that becomes tree-like with age and one of the latest flowering. It produces large, handsome leaves and funnel-shaped, almost lily-like white flowers in large trusses in mid-to late summer. Its strong, heady scent permeates the air for some distance. It prefers woodland shade and shelter, and although it may take some years to begin flowering, it is worth the wait. Height to 5m (16½ft), spread 5m (16½ft).

■ RIGHT

'SAPPHO'

A vigorous, hardy evergreen, rounded shrub. A good specimen for general planting. It produces tall, conical trusses of funnel-shaped white flowers with a striking, dark purple-maroon blotch at the base, in early summer. It thrives in full sun. Height to 3m (10ft), spread 3m (10ft).

■ BELOW

'VUYK'S ROSYRED'

Hardy, small-leaved, evergreen Vuyk azalea of low-growing habit, bred in Boskoop, Holland. It produces masses of funnel-shaped, satin-textured, deep rosy pink flowers in mid-spring. Good for a rock garden in full sun. Height to 75cm (30in), spread 1.2m (4ft).

■ ABOVE

R. THOMSONII

A beautiful, evergreen, tree-like shrub that must have stunned Joseph Hooker when he saw it in full bloom in the Sikkim Himalayas. It has handsome, peeling, fawn-brown bark with lilac shading and matt, dark blue-green leaves that are paler and glaucous beneath; after flowering, the new leaves emerge bright green before turning deep blue-green. The waxy, bell-shaped flowers are a sumptuous blood-red, taking on an extraordinary translucence as dappled sun filters through them, each bell having huge globules of nectar at the base. Hardy to -10°C (14°F), it must have shelter and dappled shade. Height to 6m (20ft), spread 2.5m (8½ft).

■ RIGHT

'WOMBAT'

An evergreen, small-leaved azalea with an unusual, dense, ground-hugging habit that makes it particularly useful for ground cover, even in full sun. In early summer it flowers so freely as to almost obscure the foliage, producing a profusion of small, funnel-shaped pink flowers. Height 25cm (10in), spread 1.2m (4ft).

■ ABOVE

R. YAKUSHIMANUM 'KOICHIRO WADA'

The parent of many modern hybrids, *R. yakushimanum* has everything. It is very hardy and sun-tolerant with a dense, dome-shaped habit and substantial shiny dark green leaves that are silvery when young: they are clothed with buff-cinnamon hair beneath. The funnel-shaped flowers are deep pink in bud, and open to apple-blossom pink, finally fading to white. 'Koichiro Wada', a selection from the original introduction from Yakushima in 1934, is still considered by many growers to be one of the best of its type. Height to 2m (6½ft), spread 2m (6½ft).

Buying rhododendrons

Before making any purchases, it is a good idea to visit specialist rhododendron nurseries and gardens to view plants in growth and flower. The peak flowering time for most is late spring and early summer. Take a notebook and jot down the names of those that catch your eye.

Many garden centres offer a wide range of rhododendrons and azaleas, and it is generally a good idea to buy locally because the plant in question should thrive in your area and climate. But if you have set your heart on a particular named cultivar or species, you will probably have to obtain it by mail order from a specialist supplier. In all European countries, the USA and Canada,

■ ABOVE
Visiting rhododendron gardens and nurseries is one of the best ways of seeing and choosing your new plants.

■ LEFT
Look for healthy plants of bushy habit (centre) without any signs of leaf yellowing (right), stunted, straggly growth (left), or premature leaf fall that may be caused by irregular watering.

■ RIGHT
Visit other people's gardens to look for attractive plant associations that you may wish to 'borrow' for your own plantings.

publications are available detailing comprehensive nursery listings. The advantage of buying from a specialist of good reputation is that, by and large, they provide plants of good quality.

Choosing plants

If buying directly from a nursery or garden centre, choose specimens with nicely balanced top growth and healthy dark green foliage with no evidence of leaf yellowing. Examine the plant carefully for evidence of any pests such as vine weevil with the tell-tale leaf-notching, or diseases such as powdery mildew. Look at the compost (soil mix) carefully and

■ ABOVE
'Johanna' is an evergreen hybrid azalea with glowing rich red flowers in spring or early summer.

make sure that it is weed-free and evenly moist – neither too wet nor dry. If you suspect that the plant has dried out in the garden centre, do not buy it, especially if the plant has flower buds, since you will almost certainly lose the flowers. Finally, lift the plant pot and examine underneath. If there is a mass of roots protruding, this indicates that the

plant is pot-bound, and may have suffered stress from drought or lack of nutrients.

Containerized plants may be found on sale for much of the year, but the best time to buy is just before you plant, in periods of clement weather between autumn and spring in mild winter areas, or in spring in areas with colder climates.

Cultivating rhododendrons

If you are lucky enough to have a patch of woodland with acid soil, the conditions will be ideal for planting rhododendrons.

Soil types

The ideal type of soil is well-drained, moisture-retentive, acid, sandy loam that is rich in organic matter. If you do not have it, remember that most soils can be made more suitable by incorporating plenty of organic matter in the form of lime-free leaf-mould, spent hops, well-rotted manure and garden compost. As organic matter decays, it produces

■ ABOVE
Testing the soil with an electronic testing kit is an inexpensive and accurate method of checking the acidity of your soil.

Soil acidity

The first and most important step when planting rhododendrons is to do a pH test to ensure that your soil is sufficiently acid. The perfect pH is from 4.5 to 5.5. If it is higher, the level can be slightly adjusted if necessary by the annual or biennial application of ferrous sulphate or flowers of sulphur. Do not use aluminium sulphate, the active ingredient of 'bluing compound', which is sometimes used to acidify soil to give good blue flowers on hydrangeas, because it is harmful to rhododendrons. If you do need to adjust the pH, it is important to keep retesting between applications to make sure that you do not overdo it. Bear in mind that you cannot make large adjustments to soil pH by chemical means without potentially damaging plant roots.

humus, a dark brown, gel-like substance which has chemical properties that help retain soil moisture. The large-scale incorporation of peat was once widely practised and can undoubtedly be effective, but because of recent concerns about over-exploitation of peat bogs, it is no longer recommended for environmental reasons.

Light, sandy soils, which drain freely and dry out quickly, need considerable applications of organic matter (50 per cent or more by volume) to help them retain sufficient moisture. On sandy soils, the annual application of mulch that is recommended as a matter of course becomes even more vital.

On heavy clay soils, which are by nature cold, wet and poorly drained, incorporating organic matter and grit is essential. The grit helps open up channels for water drainage, and the chemical properties of humus act on clay particles to form a crumb-like structure that improves both aeration and drainage. The proportions by volume need to be one part organic matter and one part grit to two parts soil. Make any soil improvements in the season before planting.

Where the soil is heavy clay made worse by poor subsoil drainage, the ideal solution is to lay land drains, but this is time consuming and can be expensive. In this case, it is worth considering building raised beds of stone, brick, railway sleepers or even hardwood logs. If your soil is also alkaline, raised beds will need to be lined with a plastic membrane to reduce contamination with alkaline groundwater to manageable levels.

Fill raised beds with specially prepared soil. The materials used can be based on composted, pulverized bark, pine needles, oak or beech leaf-mould (from lime-free soils) and garden compost with grit and good garden soil in the proportions outlined above.

■ LEFT
A purpose-built rock garden can have specially mixed soils incorporated into planting pockets between the rocks.

■ LEFT
In woodland situations, soil nutrients are replenished by annual leaf fall. Plants grown in this way need little extra feeding.

regard to sun, shade and shelter, you should match these to the conditions in your garden. It is unrealistic to plant large-leaved, shade-demanding species if your site is entirely open. Here, it is better to choose the hardy hybrids, groups like the small-leaved alpines, or some of the sun-tolerant azaleas. If you want to plant specimens that flower before the last spring frost in your area, check the location of probable frost pockets, and avoid planting at the bottom of slopes or in low-lying hollows. Since frost damage is worst where plants receive direct early morning sun, choose a north or west-facing site.

Soil fertility

In the wild, rhododendrons grow either in peaty, moorland-like soils, or in leafy, open, woodland soils rich in decaying organic matter. Because they also grow in areas of high rainfall, the soil nutrients are frequently leached away with the perpetual flow of moisture.

Rhododendrons are well-adapted to life on low-nutrient soils and do not need high levels of additional feeding, although in cultivation, where good growth and flowering are all-important, they may need a little help. If you are lucky enough to be able to grow them in a woodland area, where soil nutrients are replenished by annual leaf fall, they will not need any additional feeding.

But where this is not the case, they will benefit from a feed once or twice a year in spring and early summer. It is best to use a slow-release fertilizer, such as a proprietary (commercial) brand of hoof and horn or bone meal, and is important not to overfeed; rhododendrons dislike too much nitrogen all at once.

Choosing a site

When you know the individual requirements of the rhododendrons or azaleas you wish to grow, with

■ ABOVE
Be sure to plant where delicate flowers can be protected from late frosts.

■ RIGHT
If your garden is open, massed plantings of azaleas will provide a long season of vivid colour in spring and early summer.

If you are lucky enough to have a small patch of woodland or a stand of trees that will cast some shade and provide some shelter, you may be able to plant there with little additional preparation, but note that some types of trees are more suitable than others. You need to ensure that there is space to plant away from the immediate root zone of the shade-casting trees, preferably beyond the drip-line of the tree canopy so that adequate rainfall can reach the rhododendron root system. Also avoid planting under trees that have extensive, hungry surface roots such as limes (lindens), beeches, poplars and sycamores, since they deprive the soil of moisture and nutrients; while most conifers, and large-leaved trees like magnolias and maples, create such dense shade that plants cannot thrive beneath them.

The best types of trees for shade and shelter are oaks, which tend to be deep-rooting, or small-leaved trees such as birch that cast light, dappled shade. Do not plant beneath trees that have low branches, as they tend to cut out far too much light. If necessary, and it probably will be, prune the lowest branches of trees to create a long, smooth trunk with a high-branching canopy.

Providing shelter

Although many rhododendrons and azaleas will tolerate at least a degree of exposure to wind, nearly all do best

■ LEFT
Large-leaved rhododendrons need some shelter from cold, drying winds. Remove the lowest tree branches to admit light.

with some shelter, especially from the drying winter winds and those of early spring, which can do considerable damage to flowers and emerging leaves.

Remember that the larger the leaves, the more shelter is required, and even in a woodland site where tall trunks protect from the worst of the blast, low-level shelter is necessary. This can be created by planting shrubby, shade-bearing plants such as holly (*Ilex* spp.), yew (*Taxus baccata*) and laurel (*Aucuba japonica*), or better still, clump-forming bamboos. The ideal shelter-forming plants are those that are low-branching with some foliage down at ground level.

The same types of plant can also be used to create shelter in smaller gardens, but here a good boundary hedge may be sufficient to give protection from winds. The most important feature of any shelter is that it is permeable to wind and acts as a filter; a hedge, for example, will significantly reduce wind speed in its lee for up to five times its height. A brick wall or other solid structure, on the other hand, merely diverts the wind, usually accelerates it, and often causes potentially destructive turbulence for some distance away from the base.

PLANTING A RHODODENDRON IN A CONTAINER

1 Choose a pot that is slightly larger than the root ball. Place a layer of broken shards of old terracotta pots in the bottom.

2 Fill the bottom of the container with ericaceous (lime-free) potting compost (soil mix) so that the top of the root ball is about 2.5–5cm (1–2in) below the pot rim.

3 Place the plant in the pot and backfill with compost by trickling in around the margins.

4 Apply a top-dressing of granitic grit to help conserve moisture and to reduce germination of any weed seedlings.

PLANTING A CONTAINER-GROWN RHODODENDRON

1 Fork over the soil, remove any stones and weeds, and dig a hole 2–3 times the diameter of the root ball.

2 Check that the top of the root ball is exactly level with the surface, using a cane across the top of the hole.

Planting

Rhododendrons have compact, shallow, fibrous root systems which create a firm root ball, relatively easy to move and transplant. The usual time to plant is during periods of clement weather, when the soil is moist, between autumn and early spring. In areas with mild winters, autumn is the best time because plants are more likely to receive sufficient rainfall, allowing them to become well-established before next year's growing season. Where winters are severe, it is best to plant in spring.

3 Remove the plant from the container and tease out the root ball. Set the plant in the hole and backfill.

4 Firm in using gentle fingertip pressure to avoid damaging the roots or compacting the soil.

5 Water well. After planting, apply a lime-free mulch of organic matter at least 1m (3ft) in diameter around the base of the plant.

Care and maintenance

period of active growth, after flowering (which may be spring, summer and/or autumn, depending on variety), and especially when setting the following season's flower buds during the summer. (See also Dry bud, and Bud drop, in Pests, diseases and disorders).

Special requirements

Plants that flower in late winter or early spring also come into active growth early in the season, and this growth is sometimes caught by frost. In this case, such plants will need adequate water to develop new growth to replace that damaged by frost. For plants that flower late in the season, the growth period is correspondingly late too. The danger of drought in this case is that subsequent artificial watering may cause a late flush of growth that is so soft and unripened that it is damaged by the autumn frosts. With these species, siting them carefully, out of full sun and away from the tree canopy, where they are likely to

Water

One of the most important rules of rhododendron cultivation is that they must never be allowed to dry out. When growing in a container, it is vital to keep a constant, daily check to make sure that the compost (soil mix) is evenly moist at all times, but never waterlogged. Bear in mind that water should be applied to containers as a good soaking. Do not water little and often, as this tends only to moisten the compost surface. Collect rainwater for watering purposes, especially if you live in a hard water

area, as the lime in tap water may harm the plants.

The moisture requirements of rhododendrons planted in open ground are generally less critical than when they are container grown. Most will tolerate fairly dry conditions during their quiescent or dormant period and, even in growth, may withstand some wilting for very short periods. Do not let this happen if you can possibly avoid it, because any such stress is likely to cause a check to growth and flower formation.

Rhododendrons have their highest moisture requirements during their receive adequate natural rainfall, becomes all the more important. (If you have done your utmost to conserve soil moisture by incorporating plenty of organic matter before planting, and mulching with organic matter after planting, well-established rhododendrons will probably need additional water only in exceptionally dry seasons.) If you do need to water, this can be done with a can, hose, sprinkler, or drip-feed irrigation system, depending on the number of plants you have. Always apply sufficient water to penetrate the soil beneath the root zone. This encourages roots to grow down into the soil, rather than to remain too near the surface where they are susceptible to dry conditions.

Mulching

In nature, rhododendrons thrive in soil covered by mosses and fallen leaves – a sort of natural mulch that retains soil moisture and provides the plant with an adequate supply of nutrients. In cultivation, this needs to be simulated by the application of a mulch, about 7.5–10cm (3–4in) deep on large plants; less on dwarf species and cultivars. Always apply a mulch to soils that are thoroughly moist to some depth between late autumn and early spring. Applying a mulch to dry soils is positively harmful because it can reduce the amount of rainfall that penetrates to the roots. There are various materials that are useful as mulches for rhododendrons, all of which are characterized by their acidic, lightweight, open nature. They include matured, granulated or chipped bark, oak or beech leaf mould from lime-free soils, well-rotted farmyard manure, good garden compost, conifer needles and chopped bracken litter.

Rhododendrons as a group are exceptionally shallow-rooting, and the surface-feeding roots are responsible for nutrient and water uptake. To do this successfully, they need open and well-aerated conditions. Any mulch that forms a heavy, airless crust as it rots down, like grass clippings, should be avoided. Peat is also unsuitable.

Mulching has advantages other than moisture conservation. It helps reduce germination of weed seedlings which need light to germinate, and helps reduce extreme temperature fluctuations at the root zone. A mulch is therefore all the more vital in areas with warm, dry summers. Where rainfall is heavy, a mulch can prevent undesirable compaction or capping of the soil caused by large droplets of water.

■ LEFT
Apply a mulch of organic matter annually in spring, especially around plants that are not grown in woodland situations where annual leaf fall acts as a natural mulch.

Fertilizers

Rhododendrons are naturally adapted to soils with a low nutrient content, and have low fertilizer requirements to the extent that if grown in woodland conditions in good leafy soil, they seldom need additional feeding – annual leaf fall does much to replenish soil nutrients naturally. Elsewhere, they benefit from an annual application of a slow-release, low-nitrogen organic fertilizer in early spring.

If plants look as though they need a boost to growth, make a second application no later than early summer. If you feed later in the year, plants tend to make soft late growth that is very susceptible to cold weather damage.

Plants grown in containers should be fed in early spring and may be given a half-strength liquid feed every two or three weeks during the growing season. Do not use full-strength feed; too much nitrogen is undesirable.

Weed control

Controlling weeds is absolutely necessary if plants are to thrive, grow and flower well. Mulching helps to keep weeds down once the soil is clear, but once weeds do grow, the best and safest method of weeding is by hand, followed by applying a fresh mulch. Because rhododendrons are so shallow rooting, the surface feeder roots are easily damaged by hoes, forks and cultivators.

Deadheading

This is only practicable where there are relatively few plants; it becomes impossibly tedious where there are massed plantings. It is particularly important on newly planted specimens though, especially if they are free flowering. Removing dead flowers prevents the plant from devoting its energy to seed production, and helps promote good leaf growth and flower buds for the following season's display.

To deadhead, simply pinch out the whole truss or individual flowers using finger and thumb. Take care not to damage the growing shoot or leaves immediately behind the flower truss. It is best not to use secateurs (pruners), because it is easy to damage the growing shoots. Dwarf cultivars may have seed heads removed with a small pair of clean, sharp scissors.

■ RIGHT
Deadheading is impracticable in extensive plantings, but should always be done in the early years where possible.

■ RIGHT
Most rhododendrons need little or no
routine pruning, except to remove dead
growth or badly placed branches.

Pruning

Rhododendrons seldom need regular
pruning, but any over-long or badly
placed branches that spoil the overall
outline can be cut back after
flowering to just above a leaf node.
The only other pruning that is likely
to be needed is the removal of dead
wood in winter; cut it out near its
point of origin or back to the nearest
healthy, live wood.

DEADHEADING

1 Deadheading stops the plant putting
energy into seed production that would
be better used for new foliage. New growth
emerges below the flower truss.

2 Pinch out the dead flowerheads
using your finger and thumb to
minimize potential damage to the
emerging new leaves.

3 After the flowerhead is removed, the
point of emergence of soft and tender
new leaves can clearly be seen.

Propagation

Rhododendrons and azaleas can be increased by a number of means. Seed, when produced, is suitable for true species, but this needs to be purchased either from wild-collected or carefully hand-pollinated sources, because they hybridize freely in gardens. Because of their complex genetic complement, cultivars and hybrids do not breed true from seed.

Seed can be sown when ripe in late autumn, and will germinate quickly over winter, but may need additional lighting. Otherwise, store in a sealed plastic container, in a cool place, and sow in early spring using an ericaceous (lime-free) seed compost (soil mix) or sphagnum moss peat.

SOWING SEEDS

1 Fill a pot or half-pot with ericaceous seed compost (soil mix). Water from below by standing in a saucer of soft water.

2 Sow the seed evenly and thinly on the compost surface; do not cover.

3 Place the pot in a closed propagating case at 16–21°C (61–70°F). Seedlings usually germinate in two to three weeks.

For the amateur gardener needing only small numbers of plants, layers and cuttings are an ideal means of increase.

The hardy hybrids do not come true from seed, but many root easily from semi-ripe cuttings.

The seeds of small-leaved, dwarf alpine species germinate best at slightly lower temperatures in a cold frame out of direct sunlight.

Keep the seedlings evenly moist by watering from below. Botrytis or grey mould is the prime killer of young seedlings and plants. To reduce the risk of infection, be sure to sow thinly and avoid getting moisture on the young leaves. Grow on in an open frame in a shaded site during the summer months, but close the frame or bring the seedlings into a cold frost-free greenhouse as soon as an autumn frost threatens. The following spring, place young plants in nursery rows or containers in a cold frame, and grow on until they are large enough to plant out in the flowering site.

Cuttings

As you might expect in such a large and diverse genus, the ability of individual plants to root from cuttings and the time taken to root varies considerably. If cuttings taken at one time of year fail, it is worth trying again a little later in the season.

For most hardy rhododendrons, the most successful type of cuttings are semi-ripe to almost ripe cuttings, which are ready to take between the end of summer and early autumn. Many dwarf rhododendrons also root from ripe wood cuttings taken in late winter. They root less readily than the semi-ripe kind, but the resulting plants have a longer growing season before the onset of the following winter and so will be large enough to plant out sooner.

Semi-ripe cuttings

Take semi-ripe cuttings about 10cm (4in) long, cutting at the base of a leaf joint or node. Remove the growing point at the tip, and reduce the number of leaves to four or five. On large-leaved cultivars, cut the remaining leaves in half with a clean, sharp knife.

Wound one side of the base of the cutting by removing the tiniest sliver of bark, about 2.5cm (1in) long.

Next, dip the base of the cutting in rooting hormone preparation. Insert cuttings almost to the depth of the lowest leaves, in half-pots

containing a mix of two parts moss peat to one part of lime-free sharp sand. Alternatively, use a mix of equal parts perlite, coir and sharp sand, or an ericaceous cutting compost (soil mix). Make sure that the leaves of neighbouring cuttings do not touch or overlap. Place the pot in a closed propagating case with bottom heat at about 16–21°C (61–70°F). Keep in good light, but avoid direct sun at all times. Examine the plants frequently for fallen leaves and remove them immediately, and treat the cuttings regularly with a fungicidal drench to reduce risk of botrytis. Rooting may take place within about ten weeks.

The plants should be rooted and ready to pot on the following spring. Pot young plants into 10cm (4in) pots of peat and water with a quarter strength liquid feed at two-weekly intervals. In early summer, plant out in nursery rows or cold frames. Pinch prune the growing tip to promote branching.

The technique and treatment for dwarf rhododendrons, including Kurume azaleas, is essentially exactly the same, but the cuttings will be smaller, and they are taken in mid- to late winter. They root within 8–10 weeks. Once rooting has occurred, remove the bottom heat.

Simple layers

Layering is an ideal means of propagation if you are patient and only need small numbers of plants. It has one major advantage in that the layer makes roots while still attached to, and fed by, the parent plant. Layers can be made at any time of year, but autumn is best.

Sometimes, layers are wounded by cutting a short, lengthwise slit into the underside of the branch where it touches the soil, but rooting is usually adequately stimulated if you make a good bend in the branch. The young plant will be well rooted after two

LAYERING

1 Take a low-growing young branch and bend it down so that it touches the ground at about 15–30cm (6–12in) or so from the branch tip.

2 Dig a small hole where the stem meets the soil, about 5–8cm (2–3in) deep, and bend the stem into the hole. Anchor the stem in place with metal or wooden pegs.

3 Bend the branch tip to as near vertical as you can, taking care not to snap it.

■ RIGHT
Vigorous hybrids root relatively easily from semi-ripe cuttings.

years. Sever the branch from the parent plant about six to eight weeks before you intend to lift and transplant, to allow it to re-establish gradually.

Other methods

There is a range of other techniques that are used for the propagation of rhododendrons, but all are more difficult and less reliable than semi-ripe cuttings or layers.

The deciduous azaleas can be increased by softwood cuttings from new young growth before it begins to turn woody. The parent plant is usually brought into early growth

4 Cover the bent section with soil and support in an upright position with a cane. The young plant will be well rooted after two years.

under glass and the cuttings demand exacting conditions if they are to root and grow on successfully.

Many of the hybrids are increased by side-veneer or saddle-grafting in late summer or late winter, but this is a skilled and time-consuming operation that involves having room to grow both scion and root stock plants. Occasionally, if branches are not low enough to bend to the ground and the plant is particularly desirable, it may be increased by air layers, but unfortunately not always reliably.

The stem is wounded and packed with damp sphagnum moss, then wrapped in white or clear plastic. If successful, new roots grow into the sphagnum moss and the branch can then be cut and the layer potted up, and grown on in closed conditions.

The most modern development in the propagation of rhododendrons is micropropagation. This laboratory technique involves growing new plants in sterile mediums in highly controlled conditions, from tiny clumps of rapidly growing cells from the parent.

Pests, diseases and disorders

Aphids

How to identify: Small, sap-sucking insects form colonies on soft tissue such as shoot tips or flower buds. They can distort leaves and flowers, and may spread other diseases.
Treatment: Spray with a specific aphicide, such as pirimicarb, which will not harm beneficial insects.

Bark split

How to identify: Bark, especially on the trunk or larger branches, splits apart. Usually caused by late frost when plants are beginning active growth.
Treatment: Avoid planting in frost pockets, or where early sunlight will catch the plant after overnight frosts. Protect individual plants with horticultural fleece.

Botrytis

How to identify: A fluffy grey-white/brown fungal mass forms, and is especially prevalent on seedlings when it is likely to be fatal. Also appears on growth damaged by other causes such as frost. Spores are ubiquitous, spread by rain splash and in air currents, and they often overwinter in leaf litter or other plant debris.
Treatment: Use a proprietary (commercial) fungicide on seedlings. Remove and burn affected parts of the mature plant, cutting back into live wood with clean secateurs (pruners). Spray with fungicide.

Bud blast

How to identify: Flowerbuds do not open, then turn dry and brown to silver-grey, but persist on the branch tips. Later, a bristly fungus covered with tiny black pinhead-like structures grows on the dead buds. The fungus is spread by leafhoppers which lay their eggs between the bud scales.
Treatment: Remove and burn buds in early to mid-summer.

Botrytis

Bud drop

How to identify: Buds grow to full size and appear healthy, then drop from the branch tips before opening. Usually caused by dry conditions during bud formation at the end of summer, but may be the result of overfeeding.
Treatment: Keep plants well-watered during mid- to late summer.

Caterpillars

How to identify: Young, tender leaves are eaten and there are traces of caterpillar excrement (frass) on leaves.
Treatment: Destroy at night, or use a contact insecticide.

Chlorosis

How to identify: Leaves turn yellow between the veins. The most likely cause is lime-induced chlorosis, i.e. too much lime (calcium) in the soil which turns it alkaline.
Treatment: Avoid planting on alkaline (limy) soils. Apply a couple of doses of sequestrene as a foliar feed or root drench. Use only acidic materials such as pine needles or composted bark as a mulch.

Dry bud

How to identify: Buds fail to reach full size and are brown and dry, though the plant is otherwise healthy. Usually caused by dry conditions during bud formation.
Treatment: Keep plants well-watered in summer.

Honey fungus

How to identify: Plants fail to thrive, leaves may wilt and stems die back. The trunk base develops sheets of white fungal mycelium beneath the bark and black, shoe lace-like strands appear in the soil around the roots. Honey-coloured toadstools cluster around the plant base between mid-summer and the autumn frosts.
Treatment: Though highly infectious, some less virulent strains may be resisted by healthy plants. However, all affected plants, with as much of their root system as possible, should be promptly removed and burned.

Lace bug

How to identify: In summer the upper leaf surfaces are mottled yellow, with rust-

brown on the undersides of the leaves. Adults are dark brown, 4mm (⅙in) long, with transparent veined wings. They lay eggs on the undersides of the youngest leaves in late summer to autumn, which hatch the following spring.
Control: Avoid planting in warm, dry sites in sun. If the infestation is light, prune and burn affected shoots in early spring or, later, pick off nymphs and adults by hand. Otherwise, spray with a contact or systemic insecticide. Repeat at two- to three-week intervals from early summer.

Leaf spot

How to identify: Brownish purple spots, usually distinctly ringed with a darker line, appear on the leaves, often accompanied by tiny, black, pinhead-like, fungal-fruiting bodies. Effects are most severe on plants suffering stress.
Treatment: Keep the plants healthy by watering and mulching. Remove and burn affected leaves.

Leafhopper

How to identify: Between late spring and mid-summer

cream-coloured nymphs appear on the leaf undersides. The females lay eggs in next year's flowerbuds, which may result in a fungus infection causing bud blast.
Treatment: Control leafhoppers in late summer and autumn with dimethoate, permethrin, pirimiphos methyl, or fenitrothion.

Leatherjackets

How to identify: These grey-brown grubs eat plant roots. Usually only a pest to young plants, since they kill them by girdling the roots.
Treatment: Biological control, in the form of *Steinernema carpocapsae*, parasitic nematodes that kill the grubs, is only effective in damp soil at temperatures above 14°C (57°F).

Petal blight

How to identify: Small white or brown water-drop-like marks appear on flowers. Flowers collapse and become slimy, then dry out on the plant and re-infect blossom the next season. Prevalent in mild, damp seasons.
Treatment: Remove and burn affected flowers.

Phytopthera

How to identify: A fungus which causes small roots to rot. Larger ones show dark discoloration, as does the stem beneath the bark at the plant base. The whole plant may eventually die. Prevalent in warm, wet soils and troublesome in containers.
Treatment: Ensure good drainage, especially in pots. Remove and burn affected plants and dispose of the soil immediately around the roots. No chemical treatment is available to the amateur.

Vine weevil damage

Powdery mildew

How to identify: Brown or grey felty blotches appear on leaf undersides, with a corresponding pale-coloured blotch above. Leaves may yellow and fall prematurely. Prevalent in dry soils, the fungus attacks wet foliage.

Treatment: Pick off and burn affected leaves. Spray monthly between spring and autumn with a fungicide such as carbendazim or mancozeb.

Rhododendron rust

How to identify: Bright orange spots on the upper leaf surface appear with brown pustules beneath. Most common in damp conditions.
Control: Remove and burn affected leaves and shoots. Spray with mancozeb, or penconazole, preferably using a wetting agent.

Vine weevil

How to identify: Adult weevils are night-feeding and seldom seen. They leave irregular notches at the leaf margins. Each can lay 1,000 eggs, giving rise to legless white grubs that feed on plant roots. Plants then make slow growth, and eventually wilt and die.
Control: Biological controls are only effective in damp soil at temperatures above 14°C (57°F). Hand-picking adults by flashlight at night can reduce numbers, as can spraying them with pirimiphos methyl or bifenthrin in early summer.

Calendar

Early spring

Apply a balanced fertilizer to established plants that are not growing in woodland. Apply a mulch 8–10cm (3–4in) deep on established large-leaved rhododendrons, less on small-leaved, dwarf rhododendrons. Prune back any misplaced or over-long shoots, if necessary. Finish planting new stock. Transplant established plants to a new site, if necessary. Mulch after planting. Enjoy the first flowers of the season. Look out for pests and diseases and treat as necessary. Sow seed.

Mid- to late spring

Plan to visit rhododendron gardens in your locality, armed with a notebook. Begin deadheading early flowerers.

■ ABOVE
'Arabesque', an evergreen hybrid flowering in mid-season.

■ ABOVE
The flowering season of rhododendrons extends from late winter to mid-summer.

Early summer

Continue deadheading as flower trusses die. Apply a second feed to plants that are not growing well.

Mid-summer

Check and water container-grown plants two or three times daily in dry weather, and apply a liquid fertilizer. If dry weather is prolonged, be ready to irrigate plants in open ground.

Late summer

Take semi-ripe cuttings of large-leaved rhododendrons. Make sure that plants have enough moisture for growth and new buds.

Autumn

Take further batches of cuttings from late-ripening plants. Peg down layers of young low branches for small numbers of new plants. Improve soils by incorporating plenty of organic matter ready for new plantings. Begin the planting season in periods of clement weather when the soil is moist. Collect and sow ripe seed; store some for spring sowing.

Winter

Check for and prune out dead wood.

Late winter

Take ripewood cuttings of small-leaved and dwarf rhododendrons. Look out for the first of the new season's flowers.

Other recommended rhododendrons

'Audrey Wynniat'

'Brilliant Blue'

The heights and spreads
are the maximum that can
be achieved.
'Addy Wery' Small-leaved,
free-flowering Kurume azalea
with funnel-shaped vermilion
flowers in mid- to late spring.
1.2m (4ft) x to 1.2m (4ft).
'Audrey Wynniat' A hardy
and compact evergreen azalea
with relatively large, intense
cerise-pink flowers in late
spring and early summer.
1.5m (5ft) x 1.5m (5ft).
'Azuma-kagami' Kurume
azalea. A neat evergreen bush
bearing flowers of clear
salmon-pink, with darker
chestnut brown spotting in
mid-spring. Best in semi-
shade. 1.2m (4ft) x to 1.2m
(4ft).

'Beauty of Littleworth'
An evergreen hardy hybrid
of *R. griffithianum*, dating
back to 1900, with enormous,
conical trusses of white,
crimson-spotted flowers in
late spring and early summer.
Needs dappled shade.
4m (13ft) x 4m (13ft).
'Betty Wormald' A vigorous,
very hardy and heat tolerant
evergreen hybrid raised by
Koster of Holland. One of
the finest of the pink-flowered
hardy hybrids, it bears huge
trusses of funnel-shaped
flowers with frilled petal
margins, deep pink in bud,
opening paler pink with
darkest crimson spotting
within. 2.5m (8½ft) x 2.5m
(8½ft)

'Blue Diamond'
(*R. augustinii* x 'Intrifast')
Neat, small-leaved, evergreen
hybrid with tight clusters of
rich lavender-blue flowers,
marked purple within, with
frilled petals; they darken
with age. Mid- to late spring.
Best in sun or light dappled
shade; looks especially good in
evening light. Exbury, 1977.
1.5m (5ft) x to 1.5m (5ft).
'Blue Tit' (*R. augustinii* x
R. impeditum) Compact,
small-leaved, evergreen hybrid
with terminal clusters of grey-
tinted, lavender-blue flowers,
darkening with age. Has pale
green young leaves. Early to
mid-spring. Good for a sunny
rock garden. 1m (3½ft) x
to 1m (3½ft).

'Bow Bells' ('Corona' x
R. williamsianum) Compact,
floriferous evergreen shrub
with bell-shaped, pale pink
flowers in late spring. Young
leaves are copper-tinted.
2m (6½ft) x to 2m (6½ft).
'Brilliant Blue' This tiny,
neat semi-evergreen azalea is
tough and hardy. The mauve
flowers are profusely borne
late in the season. Ideal for
small gardens and containers.
45cm (1½ft) x 45cm (1½ft).
***R. cinnabarinum* subsp.**
xanthocodon Medium to large
evergreen shrub with elliptic
leaves. The waxy, deep yellow
flowers appear between mid-
spring and early summer.
Must have cool, humid shade
and shelter. Hardy to about

'Elizabeth'

-10°C (14°F). 6m (20ft), often less, x 1.8m (6ft).
'Coccineum Speciosum' Tall, bushy Ghent azalea with good autumn colour. Produces a profusion of faintly scented, brilliant orange-red flowers in early summer. 2m (6½ft) x 2m (6½ft).
'Crest' ('Lady Bessborough' x *R. wardii*) A hardy evergreen hybrid with shining dark green leaves. The large, bell-shaped, primrose yellow flowers are darker at the throat and are orange in bud. Mid-spring. Exbury, 1940. 3.5m (11ft) x 3.5m (11ft).
'Doncaster' (*R. arboreum* hybrid) This is a hardy, evergreen, dome-shaped hybrid with distinctive, glossy, dark green, wavy-margined leaves. The dense trusses of funnel-shaped flowers are rich crimson-scarlet and are produced in mid- to late spring. 2–2.5m (6½–8½ft) x 2–2.5m (6½–8½ft).

'Fabia'

'Dora Amateis' Compact and vigorous, a hardy hybrid of American origin with open clusters of funnel-shaped, blush-white flowers spotted yellow-green in spring. Handsome foliage and neat, rounded habit. 60cm (2ft) x 60cm (2ft).
'Elizabeth' (*R. forrestii* var. *repens* x *R. griersonianum*) Compact evergreen shrub with trusses of glossy, funnel-shaped, deep red flowers, produced in profusion in early to mid-spring. Tolerant of sun. 1m (3½ft) x 1m (3½ft).
'Everestianum' A hardy hybrid of *R. catawbiense*, dating back before 1853. It forms a dense, rounded bush, and bears handsome

trusses of frilled, funnel-shaped, pale lilac flowers spotted with chestnut-red-brown at the throat in late spring. Tolerates sun. 3m (10ft) x 2.5m (8½ft).
'Fabia' (*R. dichroanthum* x *R. griersonianum*) Broadly dome-shaped evergreen hybrid with greyish sage-green leaves, and loose trusses of deep apricot-rose flowers with terracotta tints, and brown markings. Excellent for small gardens. 1.8m (6ft) x to 1.8m (6ft).
R. falconeri A gorgeous, large-leaved evergreen species forming a broadly conical small tree. It has exceptionally beautiful new growth (clothed in dense silver hairs) that later

'Golden Flare'

becomes buff-brown. The large, pink or creamy white flowers are of substantial texture, opening in mid-spring. Must have shade and shelter. Introduced by Hooker, 1850. 12m (39ft) x 5m (16½ft) eventually.
'Fanny' Hardy, deciduous Ghent azalea with deep rose-magenta flowers that fade to softer rose-pink as they age. Late spring. 1.8m (6ft) x to 1.8m (6ft).
'Freya' A compact, hardy Rustica azalea with double, sweetly scented, pale pink flowers flushed salmon-orange. Late spring–early summer. 1886. 1.5m (5ft) x to 1.5m (5ft).
'Frome' Deciduous Knap Hill-Exbury azalea with waved and frilled, rich yellow flowers marked brilliant red at the throat. Late spring. 1.5m (5ft) x to 1.5m (5ft).
'Gloria Mundi' Deciduous, bushy Ghent azalea with

R. griersonianum

'James Gable'

'Megan'

scented, frilled, brilliant deep orange flowers with a yellow flare, borne in early summer. 2m (6½ft) x 2m (6½ft).

'Glory of Littleworth' Azaleodendron, a deciduous azalea crossed with an evergreen rhododendron to give a hardy, semi-deciduous bush. Growth is leggy and upright with attractive foliage and creamy, funnel-shaped, scented flowers with a rich, copper-orange blotch. Tolerates sun. Late spring–early summer. 1.5m (5ft) x 1.5m (5ft).

'Glowing Embers' A deciduous Knap Hill-Exbury hybrid azalea with brilliant orange-red flowers with an orange blotch. Mid-spring. 2m (6½ft) x 2m (6½ft).

'Golden Flare' A deciduous Knap Hill-Exbury azalea with large trusses of golden-yellow flowers in mid- to late spring. 2m (6½ft) x 2m (6½ft).

'Gomer Waterer' A hardy, evergreen Catawbiense hybrid

with dense, attractive, dark green foliage and huge, dense trusses of scented, funnel-shaped white flowers flushed mauve with a mustard-yellow blotch. Tolerant of sun and exposure. 2–4m (6½–13ft) x to 1.8m (6ft).

R. griersonianum
A hardy evergreen shrub becoming rounded with maturity, with soft, olive green, lance-shaped leaves, clothed with buff-brown hair beneath. The tubular bell-shaped flowers are an intense salmon-scarlet, a colour it has passed on to many hybrids. Spectacular in bloom in late spring and early summer. Will tolerate some sun. 3m (10ft) x 3m (10ft).

'Irene Koster' Hardy deciduous Occidentale azalea with charming, sweetly scented, rose-pink, yellow-blotched flowers in late spring and early summer. 2m (6½ft) x 2m (6½ft).

'Irohyama' An exquisite, delicate-looking but hardy Kurume azalea, with white flowers margined rosy lavender, each with a faint chestnut-brown eye in spring. Tolerates sun. 60cm (2ft) x 60cm (2ft).

'James Gable' ('Caroline Gable' x 'Purple Splendour') An evergreen hybrid raised in 1942, with red flowers in late spring to early summer. Flowers have a hose-in-hose formation derived from the 'Caroline Gable' parent.

'Kilimanjaro' (*R. elliottii* x 'Dusky Maid') Hardy evergreen shrub with compact trusses of chocolate-crimson spotted, rich currant-red flowers. Early to mid-summer. Needs part-shade. 2m (6½ft) x 2m (6½ft).

'Kirin' A hardy Kurume azalea, with hose-in-hose, rose-pink flowers with silvery shading, borne in spring. Tolerates sun. 1.5m (5ft) x 1.5m (5ft).

'Lady Clementine Mitford' Shrubby evergreen rhododendron with funnel-shaped, peach-pink flowers that fade to white at the centre, marked red-brown. Late spring–early summer. 2.5m (8½ft) x 2.5m (8½ft).

'Lady Eleanor Cathcart' (*R. arboreum* x *R. maximum*) Hardy evergreen, tree-like shrub with broadly funnel-shaped, clear rose-pink flowers with a maroon blotch in late spring. Tolerates sun. 4m (13ft) x 4m (13ft).

'Mrs G. W. Leak'

R. pachysanthum

'Pink Leopard'

'Loderi King George' Robust, vigorous, large-leaved evergreen shrub producing sumptuous trusses of fragrant, funnel-shaped white flowers. They unfold from neatly furled pink buds in early to mid-summer. Hardy and tolerant of sun. 4m (13ft) x 4m (13ft).

R. lutescens Elegant, semi-evergreen shrub with bronzed young leaves and large trusses of funnel-shaped, soft yellow flowers in early spring. Must have shelter. 5m (16½ft) x 5m (16½ft).

'Megan' An evergreen hybrid azalea, bred in Maryland, USA. It has relatively large, rich purple flowers from late spring to early summer. 1.2m (4ft) x 1.5m (5ft).

'Moerheim' Exceptionally hardy, small-leaved evergreen shrub with masses of funnel-shaped, violet-blue flowers in mid-spring. Good for a sunny rock garden. 60cm (2ft) x 60cm (2ft).

'Mrs G. W. Leak' ('Chevalier Felix de Sauvage' x 'Coombe Royal') A compact, medium-sized evergreen shrub producing dark-eyed, rose-pink, widely funnel-shaped flowers in generous, long-lasting trusses in mid- to late spring. Tolerates sun. Dutch breeding, by Koster & Sons, 1916. 4m (13ft) x 4m (13ft).

'Orange Beauty' Evergreen Kaempferi hybrid azalea with deep, salmon-tinted terracotta coloured, funnel-shaped flowers in spring. 1m (3ft) x to 1m (3ft).

R. oreodoxa var. *fargesii* Vigorous, hardy evergreen shrub with a profusion of large trusses of funnel-shaped, blush-rose flowers spotted red in mid-spring. Tolerates sun. 3–5m (10–16½ft) x 3m (10ft).

R. pachysanthum Mound-forming evergreen shrub with bell-shaped, pale pink flowers in spring; the new leaves that emerge are covered in exquisite, dense silver hair. 2.5m (8½ft) x 2.5m (8½ft).

'Pink Leopard' A well-named evergreen hybrid of upright habit with a profusion of sumptuous flower trusses in late spring. A relatively recent, tough and hardy hybrid. 1–1.5m (3–5ft).

'Purple Splendour' A dense, vigorous *R. ponticum* hybrid of upright habit with neat trusses of wide, funnel-shaped, rich blue-purple flowers decorated with black markings within; a fabulous colour. Late spring to early summer. Tolerates sun and is hardy. 3m (10ft) x 3m (10ft).

'Raspberry Ripple' A late spring to early summer flowering *R. yakushimanum* hybrid with large trusses of white flowers, flushed with pink graduating into a broad, deep rose-red band at the margins. 1–1.5m (3–5ft).

R. rex subsp. *arizelum* Tree-like evergreen rhododendron with trusses of large, bell-shaped yellow, pink or white flowers in spring. The new leaves are densely clothed above and below with rich chestnut brown hair. Must have shade and shelter. 8m (26ft) x to 8m (26ft).

'Shamrock' (Nanum Group) Low-growing, wide-spreading, glossy-leaved evergreen shrub that tolerates full sun. Good for a rock garden. Funnel-shaped pale

'Raspberry Ripple'

yellow flowers open from
green-tinted buds in mid-
spring. 75cm (2½ft).
'Sneezy' (*R. yakushimanum*
x 'Doncaster') Small to
medium-sized, hardy
evergreen shrub of compact,
upright habit with attractive
foliage. Freely produces dense
trusses of bell-shaped, pink
flowers in late spring. One
of a series named after Snow
White's seven dwarfs. 2m
(8½ft) x 2m (8½ft).
'Temple Belle' (*R. orbiculare*
x *R. williamsianum*) Hardy
evergreen hybrid of neat
domed habit with beautiful
green, almost orbicular leaves
that are blue-green beneath.
The whole plant is covered
in trusses of delicate, bell-
shaped, clear pink flowers
in early to mid-spring.
2m (8½ft) x 2m (8½ft).
'Titian Beauty' Compact
evergreen hybrid with loose
trusses of waxy, bell-shaped,
intense red flowers in mid-
to late spring. 2m (8½ft).

'Sneezy'

'Yellow Hammer'

'Vuyk's Scarlet'

'Vuyk's Scarlet' Hardy,
small-leaved, evergreen Vuyk
azalea of low-growing habit.
Produces masses of funnel-
shaped, satin-textured, rich
scarlet flowers in mid-spring.
Good for a rock garden in
full sun. 75cm (30in) x
1.2m (4ft).
'White Pearl' Also sold
as 'Halopeanum' and
probably synonymous with
'Gauntletti', it roots readily
from cuttings. A vigorous
evergreen hybrid with
large, pure white flowers,
spotted crimson at the
throat. Cold hardy and
very tolerant of heat.
6m (20ft) x 5m (16½ft).
'Yellow Hammer'
(*R. flavidum* x *R. sulphureum*)
Upright, slender, evergreen
shrub with small but dense
trusses of canary-yellow,
narrow, bell-shaped flowers
in early to mid-spring; often
produces a second flush
in the autumn. Thrives in
sun. 2m (8½ft) x 2m (8½ft).

Index

'Fastuosum Flore Pleno'

ACKNOWLEDGEMENTS
The author and publisher would like to thank Chris Loder at Leonardslee Garden Nurseries, West Sussex; The Hon. and Mrs Howard at Castle Howard, Yorkshire; and Chris Margrave at Wentworth Castle, South Yorkshire. We would also like to thank the following for providing photographs. Bill Ballam: 8, 9, 11t, 20t, 21tl, 21tr, 23t, 30tl, 32tl, 33t, 34t, 35tl, 35b, 37tl, 42t, 44t, 62l, 62m; and GAP Gardens: 10, 12b, 14, 15b, 16, 29r, 31l, 38t, 60m, 63b.